TOOLS FOR TEACHERS

- **ATOS:** 0.7
- **GRL:** B
- **WORD COUNT:** 28

- **CURRICULUM CONNECTIONS:** transportation

Skills to Teach

- **HIGH-FREQUENCY WORDS:** get, go, let's, the, to, your
- **CONTENT WORDS:** beach, bike, helmet, library, park, school
- **PUNCTUATION:** apostrophes, exclamation point, periods
- **WORD STUDY:** long /e/, spelled ea (beach), spelled y (library); /oo/, spelled oo (school)
- **TEXT TYPE:** factual recount

Before Reading Activities

- Read the title and give a simple statement of the main idea.
- Have students "walk" though the book and talk about what they see in the pictures.
- Introduce new vocabulary by having students predict the first letter and locate the word in the text.
- Discuss any unfamiliar concepts that are in the text.

After Reading Activities

In the book, places to ride a bike are mentioned. Talk with children about the different places they ride their bikes. How do their bikes help them get there? What kind of precautions do they take before, during, and after riding? Do they wear helmets and practice bike safety? Discuss bike safety as a group.

Tadpole Books are published by Jump!, 5357 Penn Avenue South, Minneapolis, MN 55419, www.jumplibrary.com

Copyright ©2019 Jump. International copyright reserved in all countries. No part of this book may be reproduced in any form without written permission from the publisher.

Editor: Jenna Trnka **Designer:** Anna Peterson

Photo Credits: s_oleg/Shutterstock, cover; KK Tan/Shutterstock, 1; SerrNovik/iStock, 2–3, 12 (girl), 16tr; Sergey Novikov/Shutterstock, 4–5, 14–15, 16tm; michelle_d/iStock, 6–7, 16br; Kozak Dmytro/Shutterstock, 8–9 (foreground); Thaiview/Shutterstock, 8–9 (background), 16tl; Beneda Miroslav/Shutterstock, 10 (boy); Volodymry Kyrylyk/Shutterstock, 10–11, 16bm; NicolasMcComber/iStock, 12–13, 16bl.

Library of Congress Cataloging-in-Publication Data
Names: Kenan, Tessa, author.
Title: Bikes / by Tessa Kenan.
Description: Minneapolis, MN : Jump!, Inc., (2018) | Series: Let's go! | Includes index.
Identifiers: LCCN 2018002893 (print) | LCCN 2017061694 (ebook) | ISBN 9781624969812 (ebook) | ISBN 9781624969799 (hardcover : alk. paper) | ISBN 9781624969805 (pbk.)
Subjects: LCSH: Bicycles—Juvenile literature. | CYAC: Bicycles and bicycling. | LCGFT: Picture books. | Illustrated works.
Classification: LCC TL412 (print) | LCC TL412 .K46 2018 (ebook) | DDC 629.227/2—dc23
LC record available at https://lccn.loc.gov/2018002893

LET'S GO!

BIKES

by Tessa Kenan

TABLE OF CONTENTS

tadpole
books

BIKES

helmet

Get your helmet.

3

Get your bike.

Let's bike to school.

Let's bike to the beach.

Let's bike to the park.

library

Let's bike to the library.

Let's go!

WORDS TO KNOW

beach

bike

helmet

library

park

school

INDEX